They are human too . . .

Justice has nothing to do with expediency.
Justice has nothing to do with any temporary
standard whatever.
It is rooted and grounded in the fundamental
instincts of Humanity.

WOODROW WILSON

They are human too...

A Photographic Essay

on the Palestine Arab Refugees

by Per-Olow Anderson

HENRY REGNERY COMPANY · CHICAGO, ILLINOIS · 1957

50978

THANKS   for help and cooperation in making this book . . .

To the thousands of Palestine Arab refugees who accepted me, a stranger, and who stood before my close-up cameras with graciousness rather than bitterness.

To the Arab governments which furnished me with the needed permissions to visit the camps.

To UNRWA and its director, Mr. Henry Labouisse, for transportation and advice.

To Robert Metcalfe of the *Winnipeg Tribune*, Manitoba, Canada, and Paul-Emile Tremblay of the Canadian Broadcasting Corporation in Montreal, who encouraged me during months in the Middle East.

To Mrs. Rafaelle Yates El Gredly, who did nights of typing for me in the early days of work on this book.

To my two boys, twelve-year-old Tommy and six-year-old Peter, who have not seen much of their father during the nine months he has been busy with this work.

And to my wife Sylvia, who broke into tears at her first sight of a Palestine Arab refugee camp, and brought home to me the realization that honest people everywhere fail to extend their help only because they do not know. Since then, Sylvia has given second place to home and family, to work along with me.

12 Feb 1958 Gift

On September 16, 1948, the day before his assassination, the late Count Folke Bernadotte, United Nations Mediator in Palestine, dispatched his last progress report to the Secretary-General for transmission to the members of the United Nations. Among his seven basic premises for a just peace in Palestine, Count Bernadotte listed the "Right of Repatriation":

"The right of innocent people, uprooted from their homes by the present terror and ravages of war, to return to their homes, should be affirmed and made effective, with assurance of adequate compensation for the property of those who may choose not to return."

Despite the adoption of this basic premise by the General Assembly in its resolution of December 11, 1948, the Palestine Arab refugees remain homeless, and uncompensated for the loss of their homes.

Remember, O God, what has befallen us;
*   behold, and see our disgrace!*
Our inheritance has been turned over to strangers,
*   our homes to aliens.*

LAMENTATIONS 5:1-2

DATELINE: GAZA

غزّة

GAZA

DATELINE: GAZA

Human suffering is nothing new to me. As a photo-journalist I have encountered it many times during the newspaper and magazine assignments that have taken me to seventy-four countries in the past twenty years.

But none of my experiences was more shocking to me than my introduction to the plight of the more than one million Palestine Arab refugees in the Middle East, whom I first saw in April, 1956, on my arrival at Gaza on an assignment for my Swedish magazine.

The Palestine Arab refugees exist in misery and despair in crowded camps in Syria, Jordan, Lebanon, and the Gaza Strip—in caves in Palestine, squatters' rows near large Arab cities, and the slums of the cities themselves.

I have seen the squalor of their tents and mud huts sprawled on rocky hillsides and in bone-dry, dust-blown valleys. I have felt their grief and suffering, heard their bitter memories and frustrations, and their tense and emotional cry: "Justice, justice! All we ask is justice!"

What is justice in their particular case, and why has it been denied them for so long?

When the United Nations sanctioned the creation of the State of Israel in 1948, it did not intend that the Arab population of the territory given to the Jews should be expropriated, expelled or forced to flee. But this is what actually happened. Nearly a million Arabs whose ancestors had lived for countless generations in Palestine lost their lands and homes and became penniless refugees, to make way for Jewish refugees, who had themselves been forced by Nazi persecution to flee *their* homelands.

The world has extended its help and sympathy to the Jewish refugees. Everything possible was done for them and the conscience of humanity was so stirred that it approved of their being given a Jewish state of their own.

Ironically and tragically, however, the world in attempting to right an injustice to one people sowed the seeds of injustice to another. The Palestine Arabs, whom the Jewish refugees displaced, also became victims of war and terror. For them, the world set up only a relief agency, to hand out a dole and to carry out a plan for resettling them in other Arab lands, against the wishes both of themselves and of the countries to which they were to be assigned.

Nothing has been done to answer the desire of the Palestine Arabs for repatriation to their former homes, or to compensate them for the loss of their property, or to enforce the UN-imposed boundaries that would have divided Palestine almost equally between Jew and Arab.

I cannot see why—after nine years—the world still has not solved this problem. I cannot understand how the world at large came to forget these people who, in terms of human suffering, are paying an agonizing price for a mistake for which all of us are responsible.

For, whatever way you look at it, that is the penalty imposed on these innocent people. Their grievances are real, and their cause is just. Their homes are across the armistice lines in Israel, on land that had been Arab property for more than 1,300 years. For nine years they have clung to their wretched footholds near the Israeli frontier in hopes that some day they may return.

The world has done little to give them a faith in humanity. So long as it neglects to do so they will turn to any power which holds out the promise of justice. After nine years, they will clutch at any straw.

The United Nations Relief and Works Agency (UNRWA) does what it can for them. It is not enough. The UN does not provide the Agency with sufficient funds. This admission

is revealed in UNRWA's reports to the UN—
reports that reduce the refugees to mere statistics that mean less and less to the world each
year.

It is not my purpose in this book to analyze
UNRWA's statistics or shortcomings. This
book simply presents the faces of human
tragedy I encountered in the refugee camps. It
is published in the hope that the world will
find that these people, like others whom we
have aided in the past, deserve our help and
understanding.

Suffering needs no illustration. But it must
be shown that the Palestine Arabs are people
like you and me. As our fellow men they must
be considered and treated as such. They must
be given a place in humanity.

Thus I seek to show by these pictures how
like these men, women, and children are to our
parents, our brothers and sisters, and our
neighbors.

As a Swede I am by nature a neutralist. But
this did not prevent me, along with other
Swedes, from fighting on the side of the Finns
against the Communists and on the side of the
Norwegians against the Nazis fifteen years ago.
In many ways I involved myself in the long
struggle on behalf of the Jewish victims of the
Nazis. In the case of the Palestine Arab refugees I am bound by the same feelings.

A countryman of mine, the late Count Folke
Bernadotte, was caught up in the Jewish
tragedy in Europe. He helped thousands to get
out of Nazi Germany and into Sweden. As UN
Mediator in Palestine, his recommendations
for partition considered the interests of both
Jew and Arab. He was murdered by Zionist
terrorists in Jerusalem before he could get his
plan put into effect.

In his last report to the UN Count Bernadotte said, "The Jewish State was not born in Peace as was hoped for . . . but rather . . . in violence and bloodshed."

In gathering material for this book, I chose, because of its geographical position, the Gaza Strip, a narrow bit of old Palestine wedged between the Mediterranean Sea and the western border of Israel.

Refugees here are permitted only limited travel from the boundaries of their camps. At night they are not allowed outside the camps for fear they will be mistaken for Israeli infiltrators. To guard against such attack the area is strung with road blocks, barbed wire, and machine-gun posts.

During the day a few of the refugees put out to sea to fish or to load citrus fruit aboard waiting boats. Others escape the bleak misery and forced idleness of the camps by attending UNRWA schools or by training themselves for crafts and trades they may never get the chance to practice.

The sights, sounds, and smells of the camps can never be forgotten: the billowing dust of summer and the muddy quagmires left by winter rains; the row upon row of jerry-built mud huts jammed on narrow lots off narrow lanes where human excrement mixes with the dirt; the children in their rags, and their parents clad in the traditional malayah and galabeah, peering out suspicious and hostile at strangers; the dreaded boredom of long waiting that erupts in violence as patience ebbs; the endless chant for "Justice, justice! All we ask is justice!"

It was in one of the camps in the Gaza Strip that I found Samieha, and it is to her that I dedicate this book.

SAMIEHA

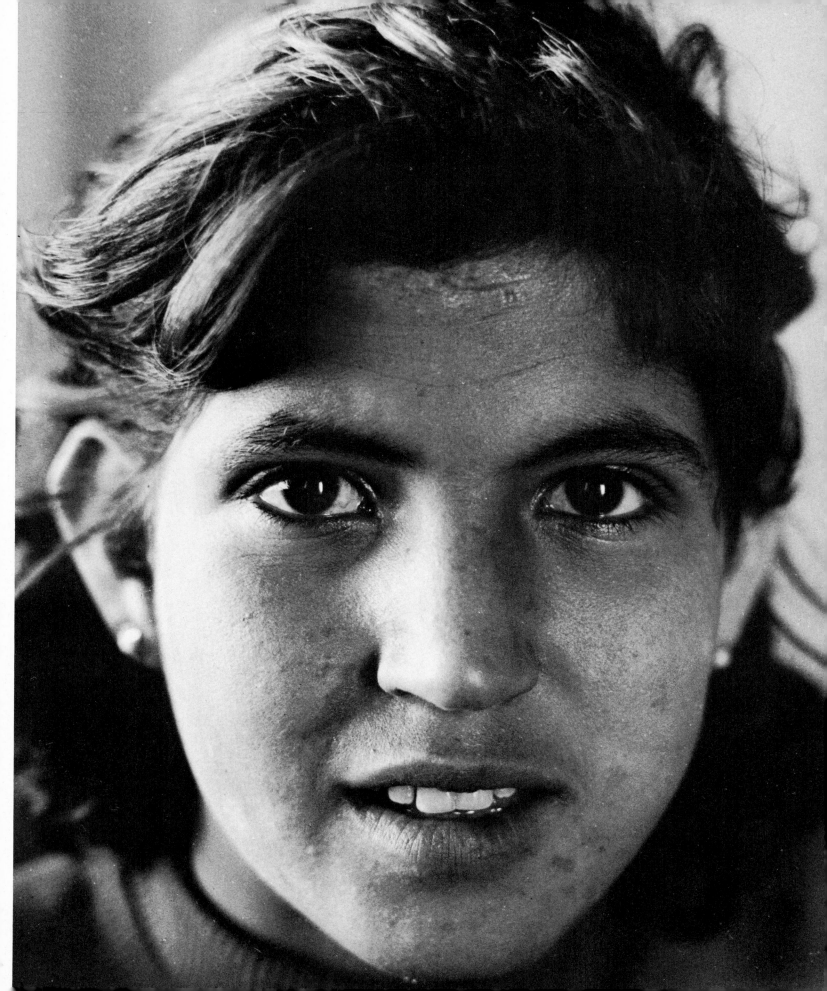

SAMIEHA

The girl stood beside a mud wall as I walked down a narrow, dusty road in a refugee camp in the Gaza Strip—a dark-haired youngster in a faded red-print frock, her legs and arms burned brown by the sun.

When I stopped, she smiled shyly, her face pressed against the rough bricks. I grinned and waved, and to my surprise she started slowly, hesitantly, towards me.

She limped, and as she drew near I saw her right foot was deformed. In the little Arabic I knew I asked her name. But the child was mute. She made only a whispering sound, and her smile faded with the effort.

People gathered around, and I turned to an old woman. "Her name Samieha," the woman said. She pointed down the road. "She live there with mother. Father dead."

I reached in my pocket, brought out a fifty piastres note, and offered it to the girl, but she drew back. Her friends watched warily as I stepped forward, placed the money in her hand, and pointed to a shawl worn by a woman in the crowd. I explained that the money was to buy one for herself.

Her brown eyes brightened; and in a typical Arab gesture of respect, she kissed my hand, then turned, and limped down the road to her home.

I had started to walk away when a woman came out of the mud hut and approached me. She said she was Samieha's mother, and she thanked me for the gift to her daughter. I questioned her about the girl, and she said that Samieha was fourteen and that she had lost her power of speech two years after the family was forced to leave their home in Palestine in 1948.

An American doctor in Gaza city, she said, was certain that operations could straighten

Samieha's leg and possibly give her back her voice. But the operations were expensive, and under the present circumstances the family saw little hope of raising the money. The woman's eyes clouded when she spoke of Samieha. As we talked, the girl herself appeared in the doorway of her home, and I felt her watching me.

But it was getting late, and I had a great deal of work to do before nightfall. I said goodbye to Samieha and her mother and continued my tour of the camp.

For the rest of the afternoon I took pictures of children at play, at school, or with their mothers, of old people sitting quietly in the shade of coffee houses, of young men and boys learning trades, and of young women hunched over their intricate needlecraft.

But I could not forget the girl with the crippled leg and the voice that was barely a whisper.

At the tuberculosis hospital I asked the resident doctor about Samieha. He was not familiar with her case, but he suggested I see a Dr. Young at the American Baptist Hospital in the city of Gaza. I decided to take Samieha with me.

Her mother at first was reluctant to let the child go. Finally she agreed, but only if her son, a boy about sixteen, accompanied us. By Arab standards, Samieha was of marriageable age, and such girls do not walk abroad alone with strangers. The three of us drove to Gaza in a UNRWA car.

I found Dr. Young at the Baptist Hospital, told him of my interest in Samieha, and asked if anything could be done for her. He examined her briefly and advised me that surgery could indeed straighten her leg. The deformity, he said, was caused by an injury to the upper thigh, possibly when she was a child.

But he could give no such definite hope for her voice. He believed Samieha's best hope was an operation by a specialist in the United States, and he offered to make inquiries if I thought there was a possibility of getting Samieha to America.

During our conversation Samieha watched us closely. Apparently she understood we were discussing her. When I asked Dr. Young about Samieha's chances of receiving the operations in Gaza, he shook his head, and Samieha turned away.

Tears were in her eyes, and I brushed them away with the back of my hand. I thanked Dr. Young, and placing my arm around her frail shoulders, I walked with her out of the hospital. In the courtyard a group of young children, laughing and joking, skipped along beside us. She turned her head into my jacket.

Outside, I left Samieha with her brother and made clear I would see them "bocra" (tomorrow). When I waved goodbye from the car, Samieha smiled, but her eyes sparkled with tears.

I got out of the car and walked over to her. At the moment, I could not speak. I kissed her lightly on her cheek, walked back to the car, and drove off.

Next day, I visited Samieha's home to say farewell to this child whom I had come to think of as a daughter. My mind was already made up. Of all the thousands of refugees who needed the help and understanding of the outside world, this girl would be my special care.

The same day I flew to Cairo, then on to my wife and two boys in Sweden. I did not see Samieha for two months, until I returned to Gaza with my wife Sylvia.

While on assignment in Gaza, where I first encountered the terrible plight of the Palestine Arab refugees, an idea was born for a picture book on these suffering people. Sylvia and I decided that my profits from such a book would go toward the cost of Samieha's operations, and possibly her schooling in the United States.

When we got to Gaza and to Samieha's camp, Sylvia, shocked into tears by the conditions in which the people lived, was immediately drawn to the girl. During our week's stay at Madam Nasar's hotel, she took Samieha to the hairdresser, bought her lingerie, shoes, and an outfit of clothes such as the girl had never known. Samieha was delighted, and she clung close to Sylvia in our visits to Gaza refugee camps. And when Sylvia gave her a Parisian jumper the day we left, Samieha was overwhelmed. Her eyes sparkled with hope and gratitude when we said goodbye.

We had intended to return for Samieha in two months and to bring her to Cairo. Then the three of us were to fly to the United States to arrange publication of this book and, subsequently, the operations for Samieha.

But on October 29, 1956, while Sylvia and I waited for our plane at El Arish, the Egyptian military airport in Sinai, word came by phone that Israeli forces were advancing from their borders against Egypt. We flew to Cairo, and Sylvia six weeks later returned to Stockholm. I covered the war in Sinai and the Anglo-French invasion of Port Said for the International News Service.

We have not heard from the UNRWA officials at Gaza who had promised to keep us informed about Samieha. Our only conclusion is that the war and the long occupation of the Gaza strip by Israel have prevented them from doing so. Today we are working through UNRWA to have Samieha brought out of her shabby world to join us in America.

Though it is months since we last saw her in the camps of the Palestine Arab refugees, we feel this child who came to mean so much to us knows we have not forgotten her.

And I am praying God on high,
And I am praying Him night and day,
For a little house — a house of my own —
Out of the wind's and rain's way.

PADRAIC COLUM

19

آمَنْتُ بِاللَّه

AMENT B'ALLAH

آمَنْتُ بِاللَّه

AMENT B'ALLAH

Through my meeting with Samieha and because of the affection and compassion I felt for this crippled child, I was given a chance to do something for the Palestine Arab refugees.

And Samieha—in spite of her handicap, or because of it—was given reason to place her childish faith in humanity.

Almost half of the one million refugees are, like Samieha, children under fifteen. She had the promise of escape from her gray, monotonous world with its bleak heritage of angry frustrations; and this promise alone erased much of the bitterness around her. The same promise could be held out for others like her.

But the old people in the land of the living dead no longer expect their fellow men to deliver them from their suffering. Their tragedy came home to me in a winding alley in the Beach Camp of Gaza.

While taking pictures for the story of the Arab refugees, I walked there one day in the autumn of 1956 with an Arab friend.

In front of a mud hut an elderly, gray-bearded Arab squatted in his rags. The sharp contrast of his beard, white hair, and brown skin gave him a strangely ethereal look and an appearance of peace. Beside the door and slightly above his head was a simple pasteboard bearing a line from the Holy Koran. The words in Arabic—AMENT B'ALLAH—I had seen a few months before above a barbershop doorway in Mount Hussein Camp outside Amman, Jordan.

At that time the Arabic had been read to me. Now I recognized the lettering, but I still did not know its significance. I stopped, and the old gentleman gazed at me frankly and kindly.

I turned to my friend and asked him the meaning of the words.

"It means 'In God I have Faith,'" he said. "Many of these people display the sign inside and outside their homes and shops."

I walked over to the old fellow and greeted him. He smiled slightly and got slowly to his feet. We shook hands. Through my companion, I asked if he saw any hope of a solution to the problem of the Palestinian Arab refugees.

He looked at me for a long moment. "Nine years ago we had hope in humanity. We were forced to leave our homes, but we thought it was only for a little while. We were told—and we believed—they would be returned to us. But after nine years many of us are losing hope, and some"—he looked at the sign wedged in the cornshocks by his doorway—"even our faith in God."

He squinted in the sun. "You see, whether we are Christians or Moslems, the Palestine Arabs cannot understand the Jewish claim to our country. We find it unbelievable that the Jews should claim it on the grounds that they lived here two thousand years ago, or that they are the chosen people of God. Are we not all children of God? Has one religion the right to claim custody of this Holy Land that is looked upon with equal reverence also by Christians and Moslems?"

I started to answer, but he held up his hand. "It is a sad thing, too, that the Jews and Arabs, who have lived in peace for hundreds of years, have become enemies because of this Zionist ambition to have a country of their own. We have become refugees on the borders of our own country to make room for other refugees from many parts of the world. The Jewish refugees should be the first to understand our persecution. We are homeless people living in these camps within sight of our rightful homes. Is it any wonder we become more bitter as each year passes with nothing done?"

As he talked I thought of others like him in the camps of the refugees. For I had met many such people.

. . . In border villages where some exist on UNRWA rations, within sight of their former farms and orange groves across the no man's land in Israel.

. . . In unorganized camps where there are no rations, and refugees must beg from other refugees.

. . . In camps in Jordan's Hebron hills where some are too enfeebled to raise the tents that collapse about them in storms.

. . . In run-down rooms in Beirut slums where those who were at first too proud to accept UNRWA handouts have finally exhausted their savings and now are forced to seek help.

. . . In fly-ridden coffee houses in camps in Syria where they sit day after day with old cronies and talk endlessly of the past and the injustice done them.

Their only escape is the cemeteries lying outside the camps on patches of sandy soil and hillsides where strangely built headstones will mark their last sleep.

The old Arab did not see the possibility of returning to his olive groves in Palestine. "We have lost everything. We can only sit and wait for somebody to give us justice. Those like me will very likely die here."

And the others?

"We are leaving our children in the hands of God. We hope and pray they will be spared to return to the life we once knew. Here they are born to life in a ghetto. They must be given a chance of freedom and happiness.

"If the world wants to prove its faith in humanity, justice, and the United Nations, then it must support the cause of the Palestine Arab refugees."

He turned again to his sign by the doorway. "I believe in these words from the Holy Koran," he said in Arabic.

"In God I have Faith."

The old man in the Beach Camp of Gaza still clings to his trust in God's will. Samieha, with youth on her side, has placed her trust in man.

I myself can only trust that the world will accept its responsibility toward these desolate and innocent victims of our questionable actions.

With my pictures I introduce you to some of those I met in the camps of the Palestine Arab refugees.

People like the women and children waiting patiently for food rations . . .

a sad-eyed, patriarchial graybeard behind barbed wire . . .

a family walking down a dusty road outside a Gaza camp . . .

a smiling woman carrying a bundle of laundry . . .

a child leading her blind grandmother down a narrow walk . . .

a little schoolgirl gazing shyly into my camera . . .

a mischievous child in pigtails . . .

a young girl awaiting the Black Angel in a TB-hospital ward . . .

When I showed my Palestine Arab friends the pictures I had taken of them, they often pointed out my face reflected in their own eyes on the photographic prints. "Yes," they would say, "a man is reflected in another man's eyes." In the pages that follow, rather than telling you about these people, I ask you simply to look at them. They will look back at you; and I believe that as you look into their eyes, you will, as I did, see yourself:

They are human too . . .

. . . rash little boys who stay alive by luck,
And Heaven's favor in this world of tears.

ARTHUR GUITERMAN

Blessed be the hand that prepares a pleasure for a child,
for there is no saying when and where it may bloom forth.

DOUGLAS JERROLD

Then the Lord God said:

"It is not good that the man should be alone;

I will make him a helper fit for him."

GENESIS 2:18

You must look into people as well as at them.

LORD CHESTERFIELD

. . . the law of retaliation is ordained you for the slain;
the free shall die for the free
the servant for the servant and woman for the woman.

THE KORAN

38

Many shall run to and fro,
and knowledge shall be increased.

DANIEL 12:4

The prayers of an old man
are the only contributions
left in his power.

THOMAS JEFFERSON

Of morals, classes, business, war, this child
Knew nothing. We were pardoned when he smiled.

DAVID GASCOYNE

"Salaam Aleikum"

    The peace of God abide with you.

Money is very slow to come where there is poverty.

SENECA

Why should there not be a patient confidence
in the ultimate justice of the people?
Is there any better or equal hope in the world?

ABRAHAM LINCOLN

54

Mother is the name for God
in the lips and hearts
of little children.

WILLIAM MAKEPEACE THACKERAY

It is work which gives flavor to life.

Mercy has a human heart— Pity a human face . . .

WILLIAM BLAKE

A dog has looked at you,
          you answer for its glance,
A child has clutched your hand,
          you answer for its touch,
A host of men moves about you,
          you answer for their need.

MARTIN BUBER

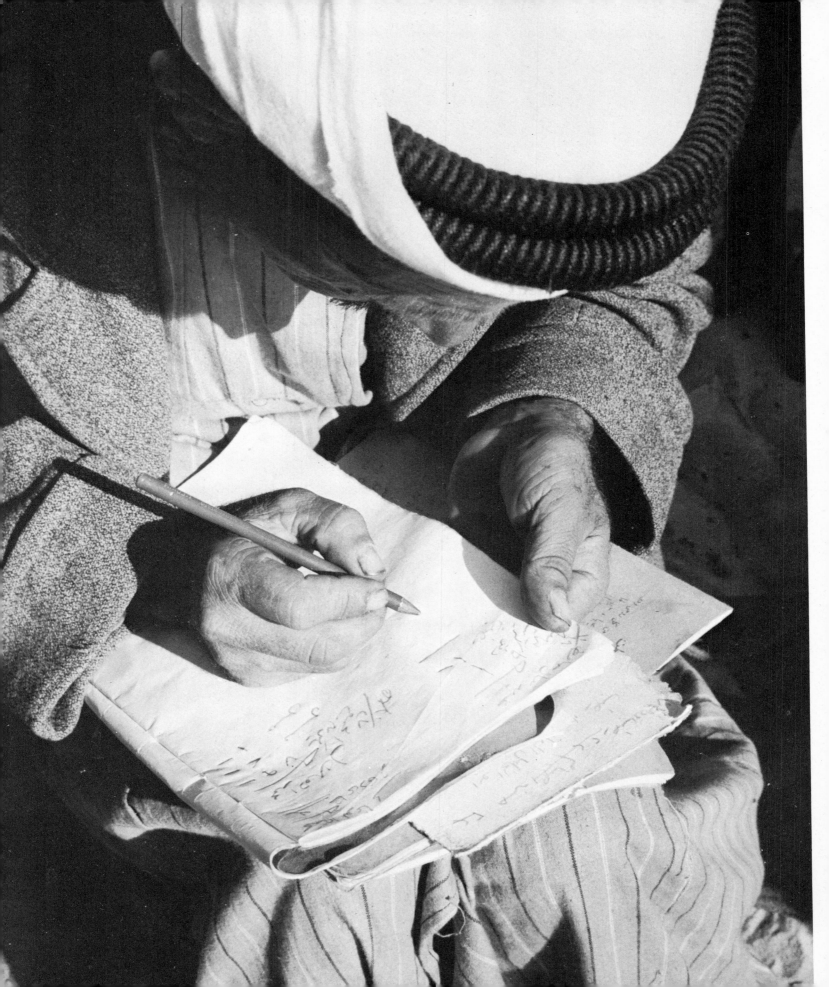

... *in order that man may not be lost*
there is need of persons who are not collectivized
and of truth which is not politicized.

MARTIN BUBER

The way to do — is to be.

LAO TZU

Patience is the key of content.

MOHAMMED

Who is the Slayer?
Who the Victim?
Speak!

SOPHOCLES

*Education is an ornament in prosperity
and a refuge in adversity.*

ARISTOTLE

Dwelling upon the trivial so long,
and spinning allegory out so thin . . .

LEON BACON

Man is carrier of Life, and God alone is Life.

EMANUEL SWEDENBORG

I think of thee with many fears
For what may be thy lot in future years.

CHRISTOPHER WORDSWORTH

Only he who himself turns
        to the other human
and opens himself to him,
        receives the world in him.

MARTIN BUBER

One's eyes are what one is,
One's mouth what one becomes.

. . . whenever we come near one another,
. . . we are bound up in relation to the same centre.

MARTIN BUBER

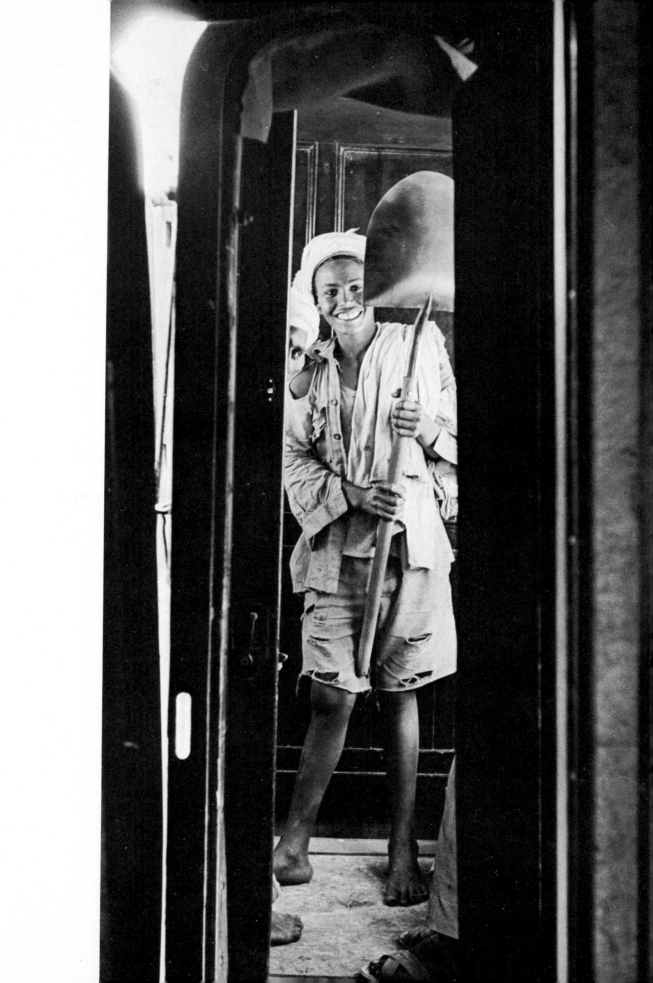

And before him shall be gathered all nations;
and he shall separate them one from another,
as a shepherd divideth his sheep from the goats.

MATTHEW 25:32

Once we and our brothers traveled on this road—
from their home to ours, from ours to theirs.
Now the road is broken, and the journey ends at nowhere.
So do we . . . .

The greatest poem ever known
Is one all poets have outgrown:
The poetry, innate, untold,
Of being only eight years old.

CHRISTOPHER MORLEY

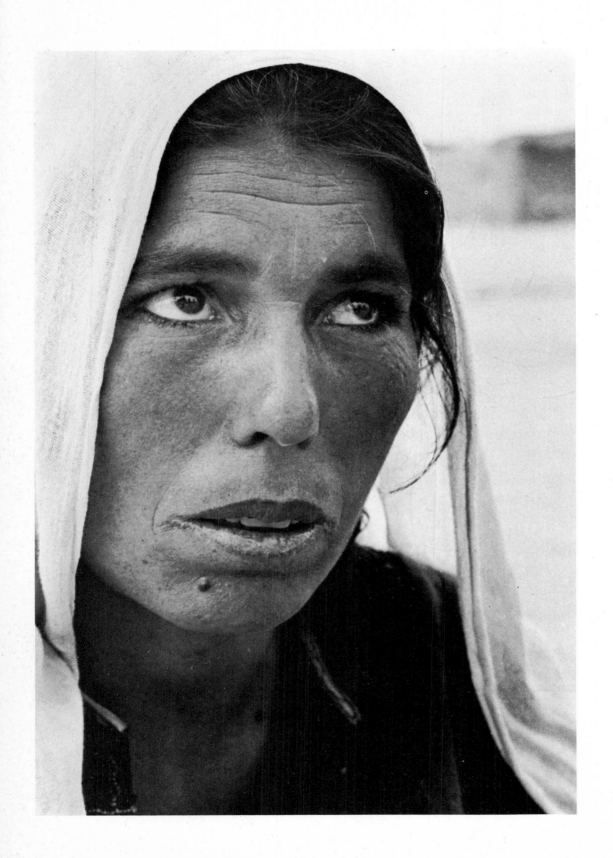

It is a comfort
to the unhappy
to have companions
in misery.

BENEDICT SPINOZA

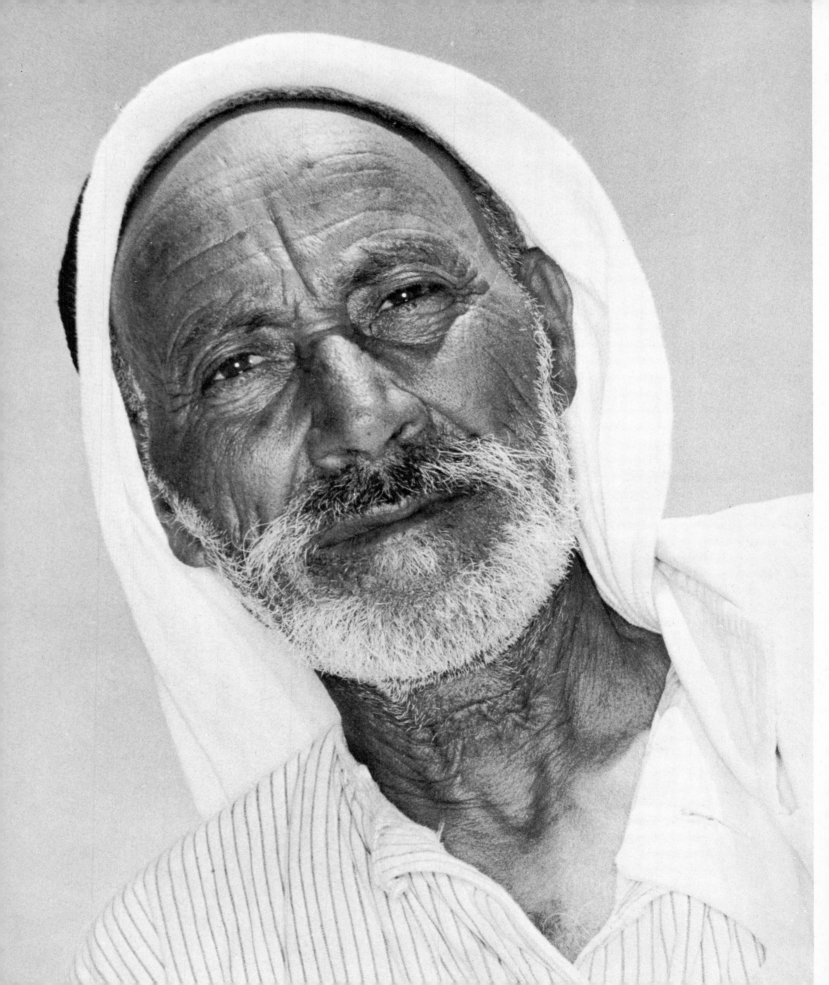

True charity is the desire
to be useful to others
without thought of recompense.

EMANUEL SWEDENBORG

The woman said to him:
*"Sir, give me this water,
that I may not thirst."*

JOHN 4:15

Now deep in ocean
sunk the lamp of light
And drew behind the cloudy
veil of night.

HOMER

*It would be far better to work at the prevention of misery,
than to multiply places of refuge
for the miserable.*

DENIS DIDEROT

Who knows the thoughts of a child?

NORA PERRY

The pearl of Justice is found in the Heart of Mercy.

ST. CATHERINE OF SIENA

I do be thinking God must laugh
The times He makes a boy;
All element the creatures are,
And devilment and joy.

WINNIFRED M. LETTS

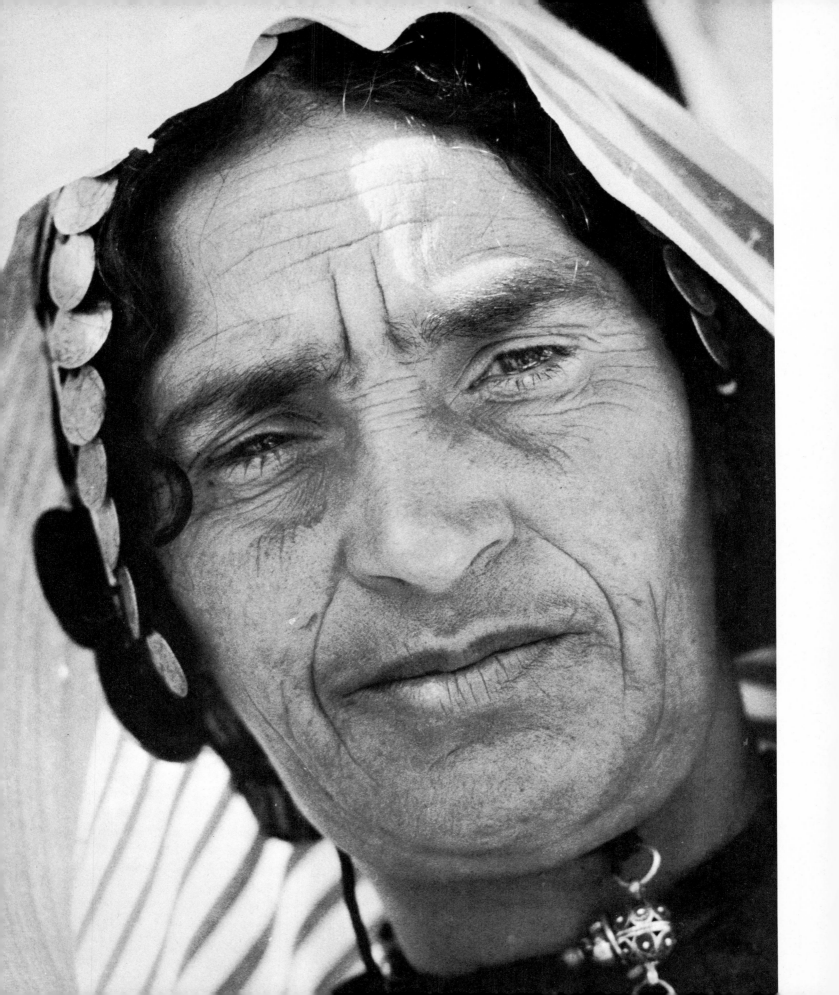

Saepe tacens vocem verbaque vultus habet.
— Often a silent face has voice and words.

OVID

Speak to me, I am blind and poor —
I never had to beg before . . .

UNKNOWN

All is fish that comes to the net . . .

SWEDISH PROVERB

Preach to the storm,
and reason with despair,
But tell not Misery's son
that life is fair.

HENRY KIRK WHITE

All fish are not caught with flies.

JOHN LYLY

The memory of the just is blessed;
but the name of the wicked shall rot.

OLD TESTAMENT

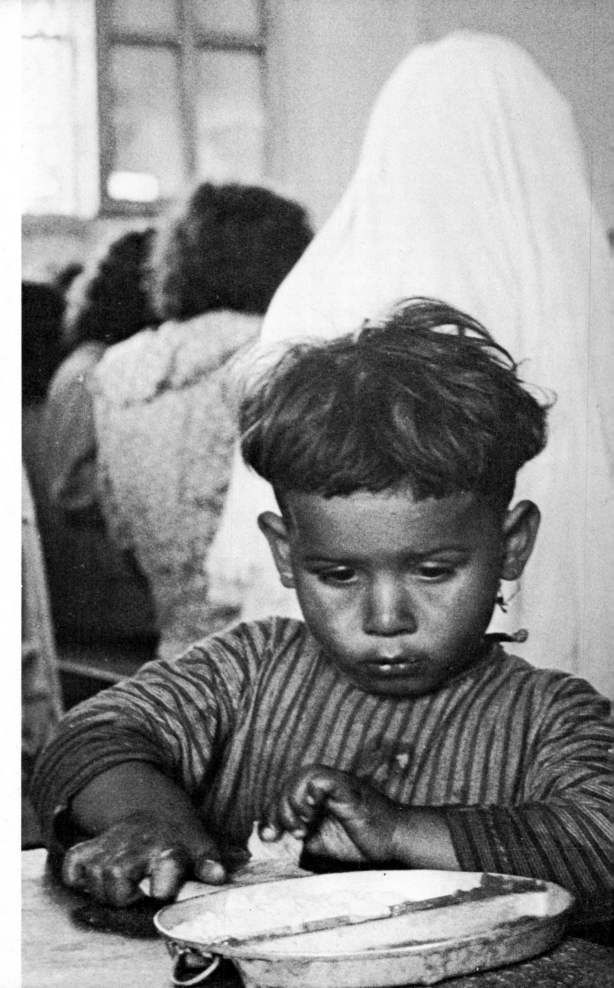

Such is;
What is to be?

FRANCIS THOMPSON

Give a little love to a child,
and you get a great deal back.

JOHN RUSKIN

If God has spoken,
    why is the universe not convinced?

PERCY BYSSHE SHELLEY

*Motherhood is the keystone of the arch
of matrimonial happiness.*

THOMAS JEFFERSON

I feel in every smile a chain . . .

JOHN WOLCOT

... that my weak hand
    may equal my firm faith.

HENRY DAVID THOREAU

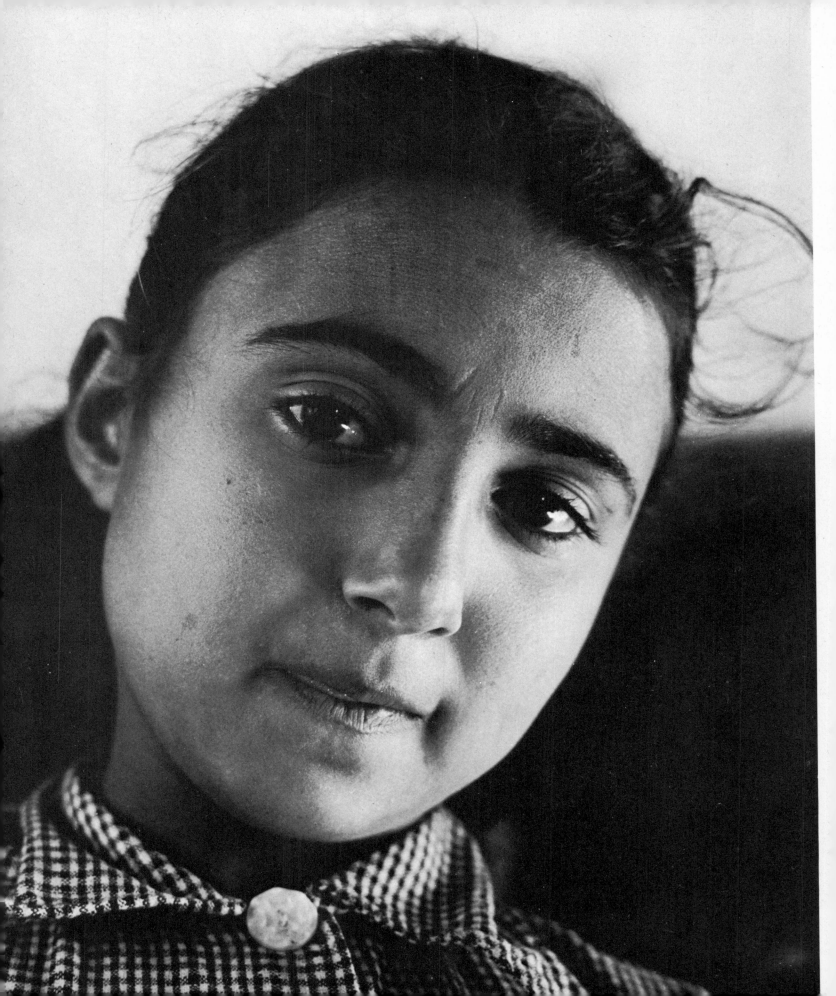

Life is a sweet and joyful thing
for the one who has someone to love
and a pure conscience.

LEO TOLSTOY

One hair of a woman
can draw more than
a hundred pair of oxen.

JAMES HOWELL

Life and misery began together.

THOMAS FULLER

149

I walk between
    darkness and light—
the night of exile and
    the shining memory of home.
The land I knew
    is given up to strangers.
There, in the sunshine,
    do they feel my shadow?

*It is hard for the happy
to understand misery.*

QUINTILIAN

Patience is bitter —
but its fruit is sweet.

JEAN-JACQUES ROUSSEAU

157

I shall welcome death
As princes do some great ambassadors.

JOHN WEBSTER

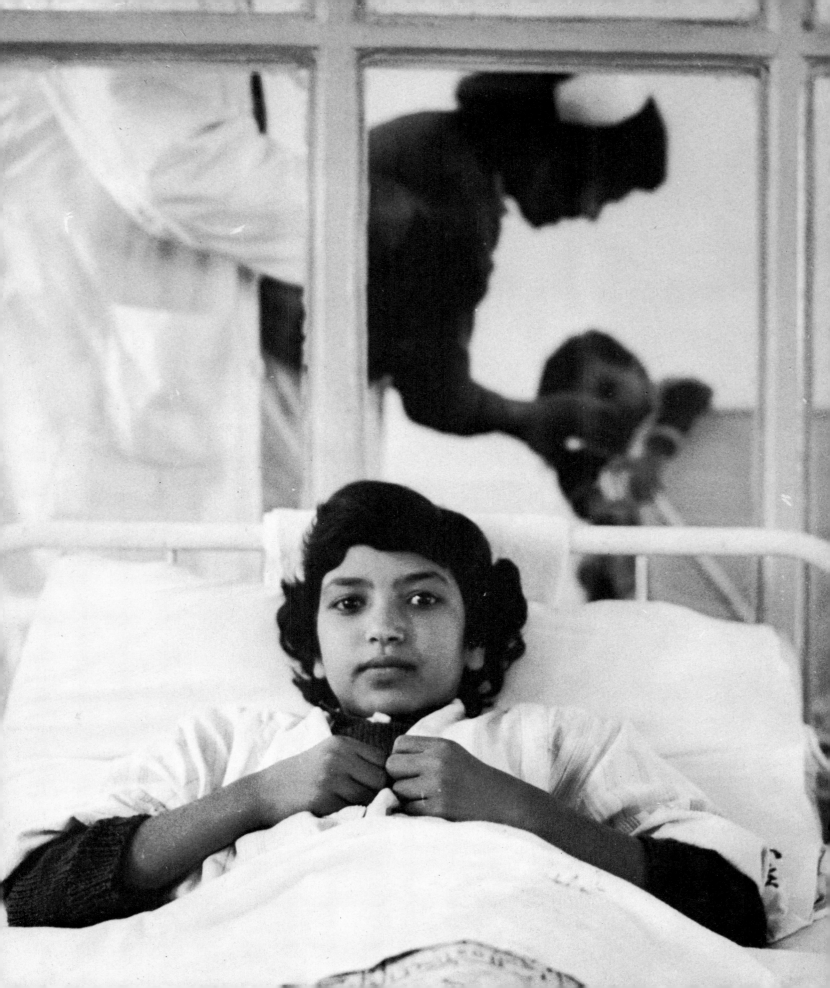

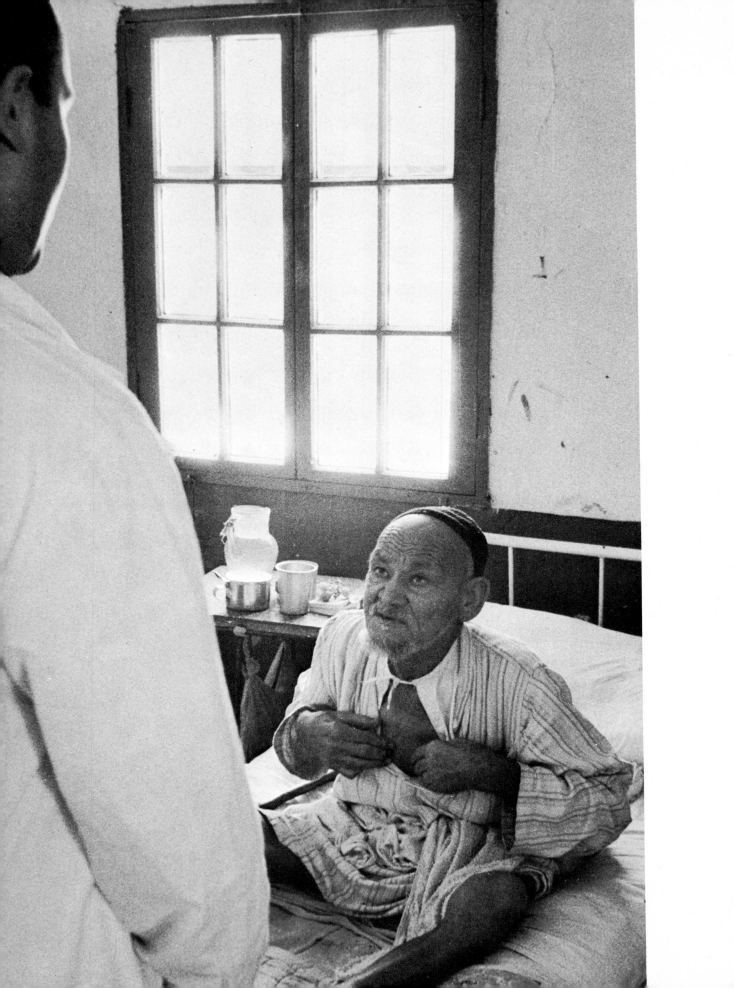

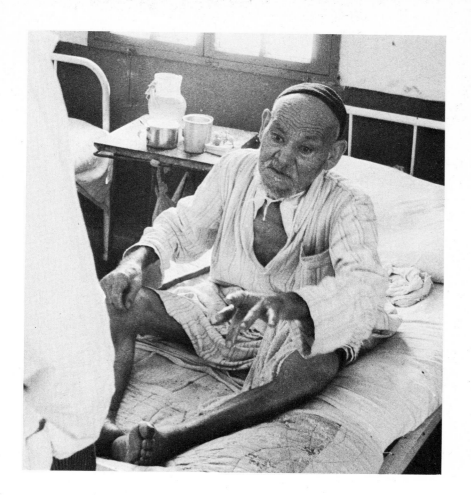

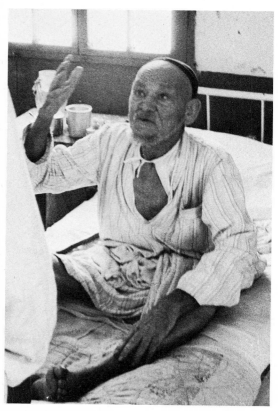

Let us go over the river,
and sit in the shade of the trees . . .

T. J. JACKSON

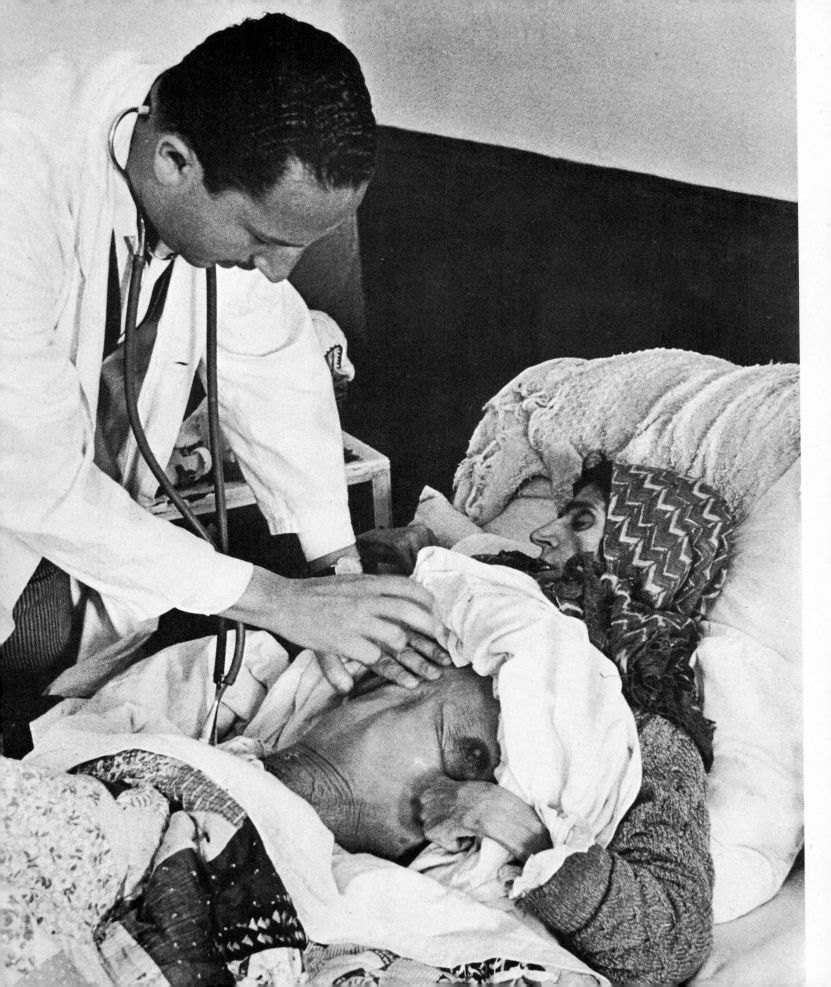

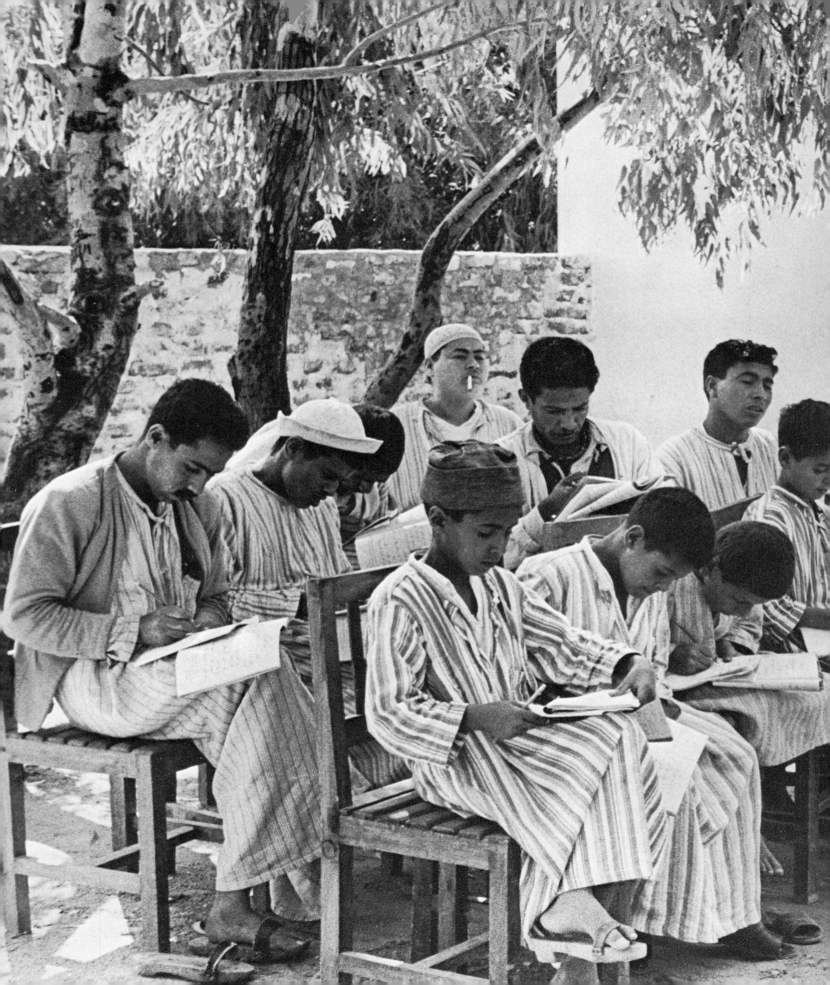

Nihil honestum esse potest,
quod justitia vacat.
— Nothing that lacks of justice
can be morally right.

CICERO

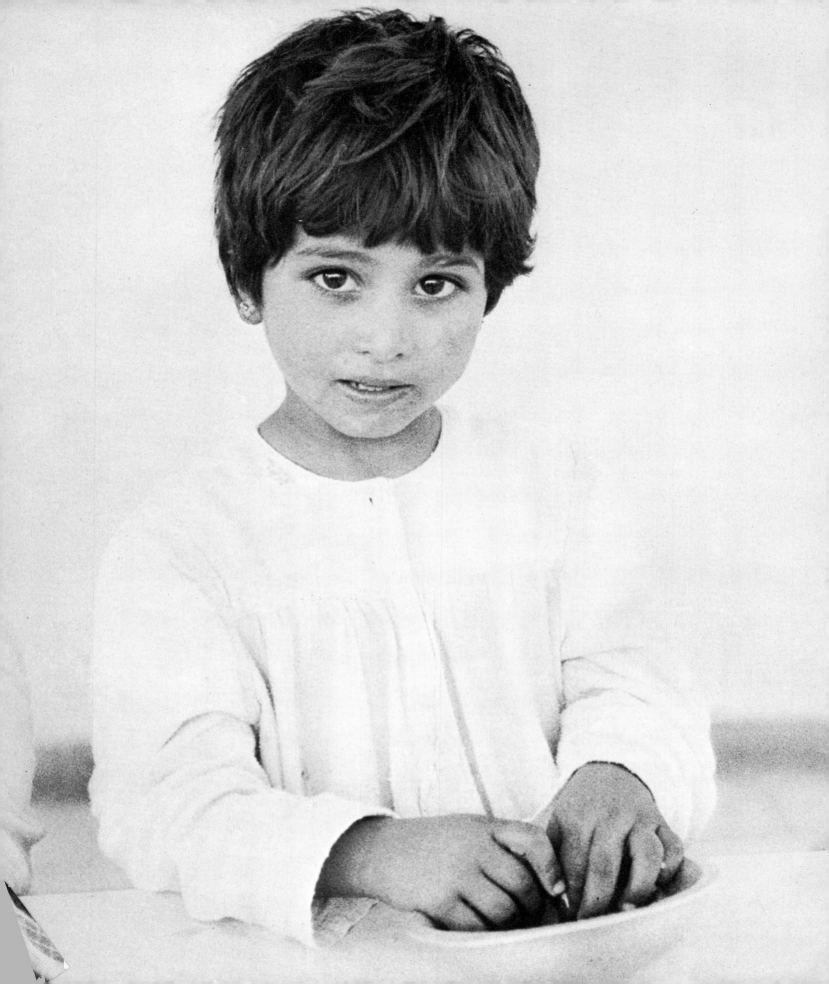

It were better for him that a millstone were hanged about his neck,
and he cast into the sea, than that he should offend
one of these little ones.

LUKE 17:2

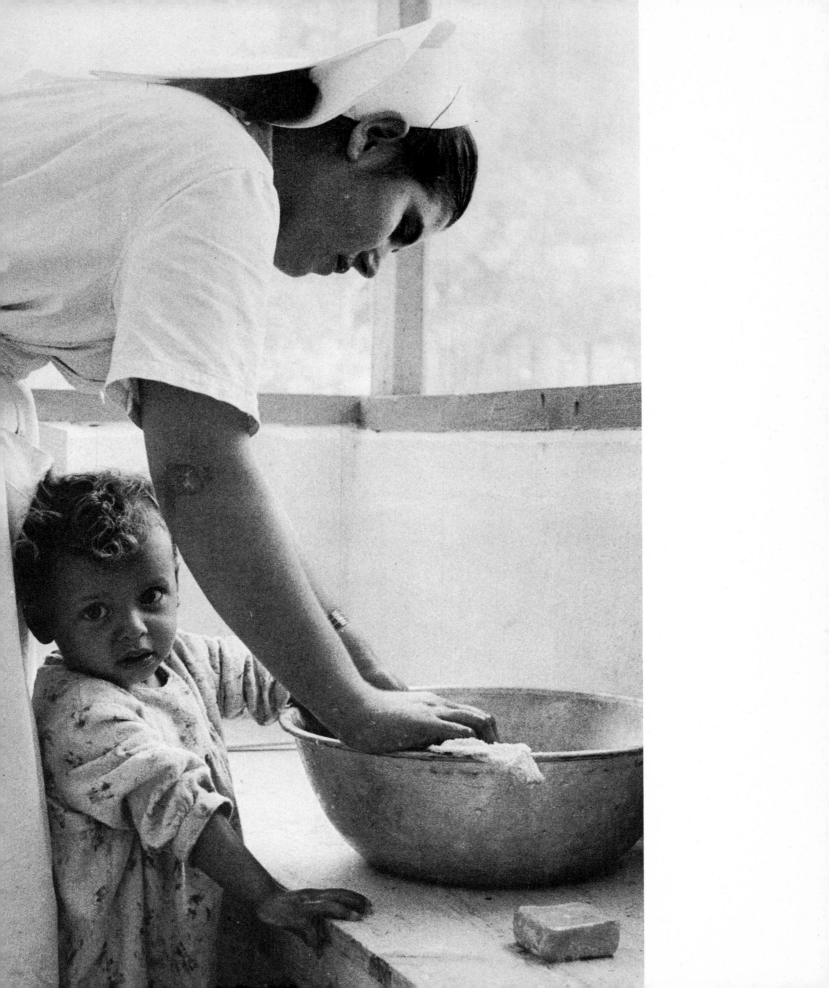

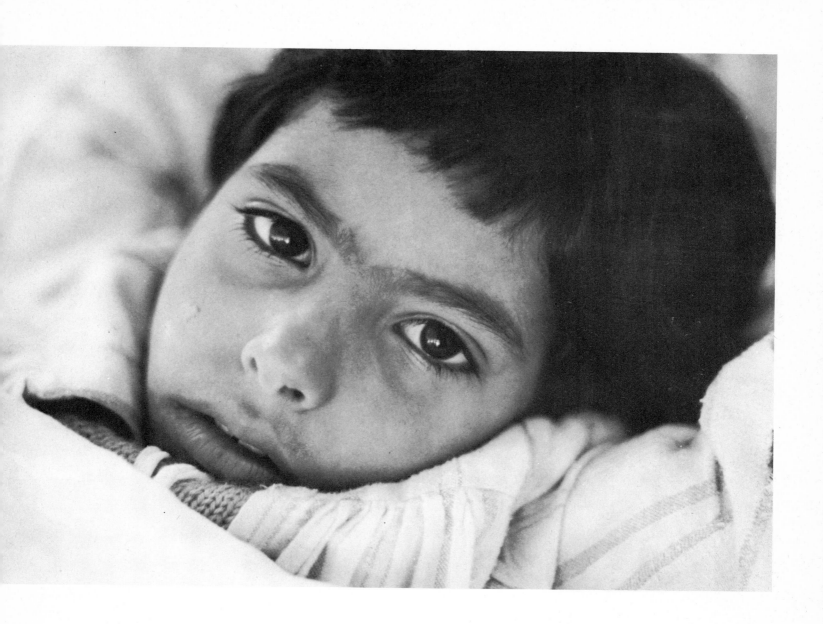

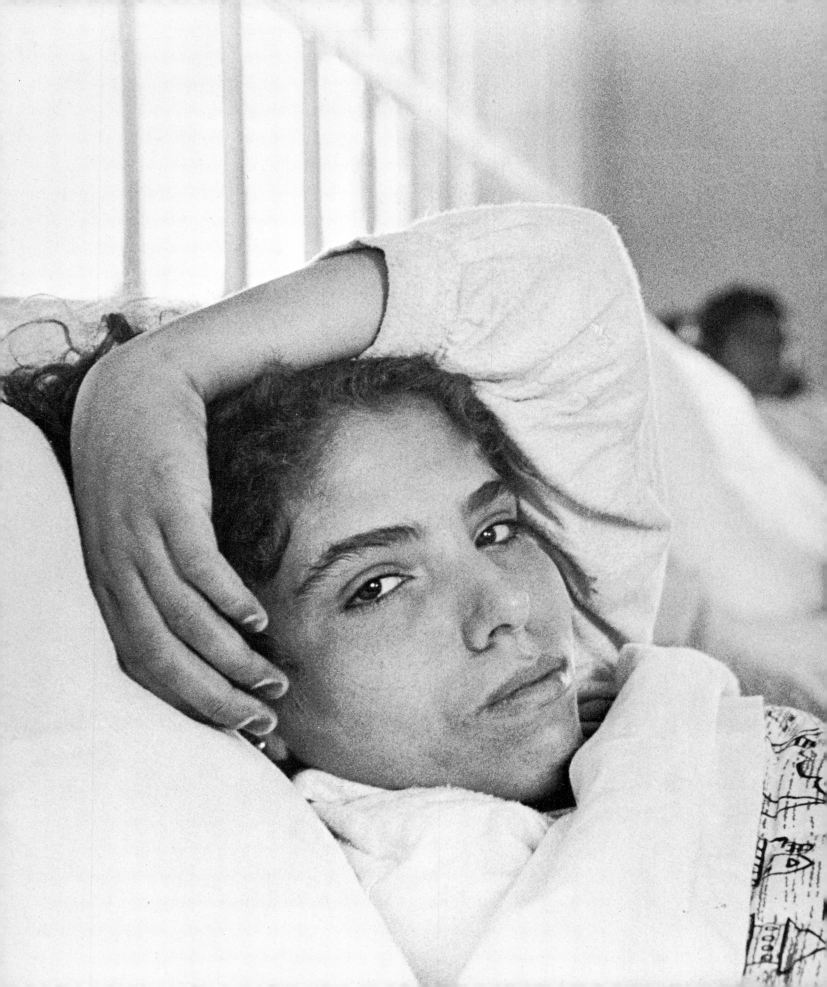

The hour of departure has arrived,
and we go our ways—
I to die, and you to live.
Which is the better. God knows.

PLATO

. . . the very first thing that cannot be denied
is the right of others to live.

ALBERT CAMUS

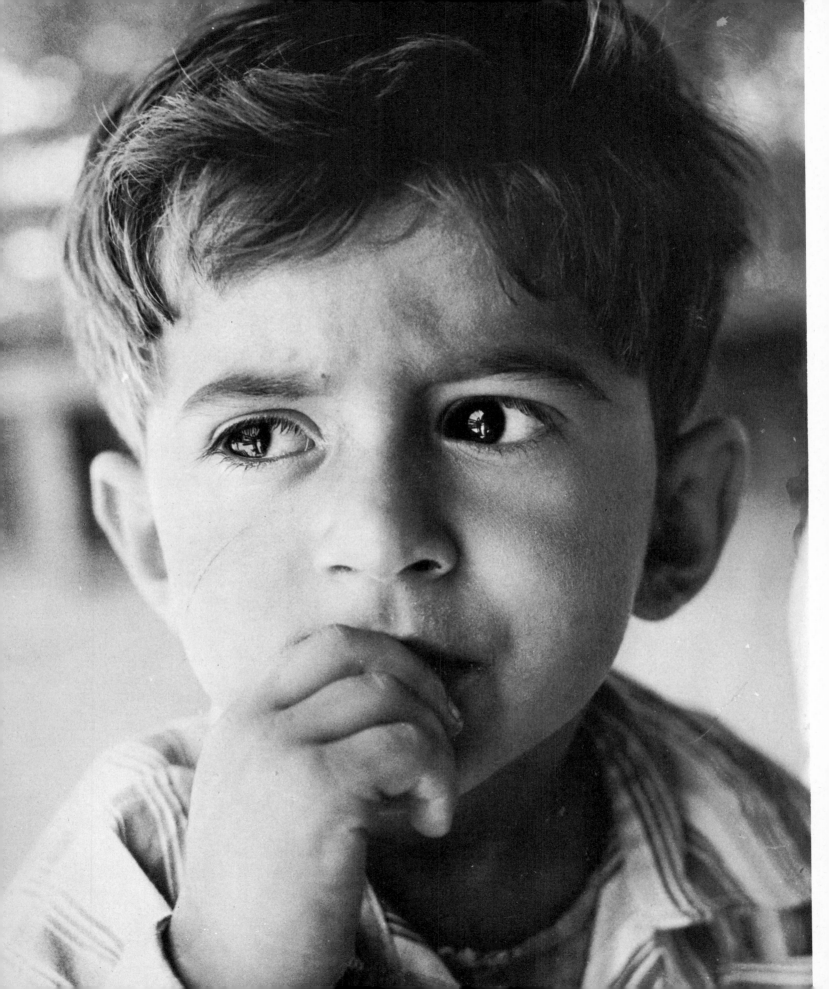

Eyes can speak
and eyes can understand.

GEORGE CHAPMAN

*All the knowledge in the world
is not worth a child's tears.*

FEODOR DOSTOIEVSKY

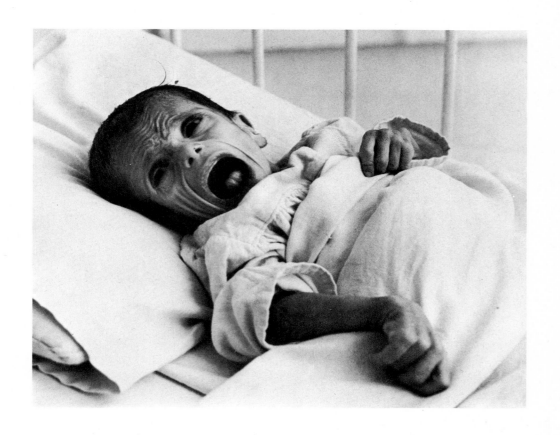

Life is the desert, Life is the solitude,
Death joins us to the great majority.

EDWARD YOUNG

A voice was heard in Ramah,
wailing and loud lamentation,
Rachel weeping for her children;
she refused to be consoled,
because they were no more.

MATTHEW 2:18

PALESTINE ARAB REFUGEES

GAZA STRIP:		217,000
JORDAN:		513,600
SYRIA:		94,000
LEBANON:		103,000
	TOTAL	927,600

These figures represent the number of
Palestine Arab Refugees registered with
UNRWA . . . out of a total of 1,152,000
PALESTINE ARAB REFUGEES.

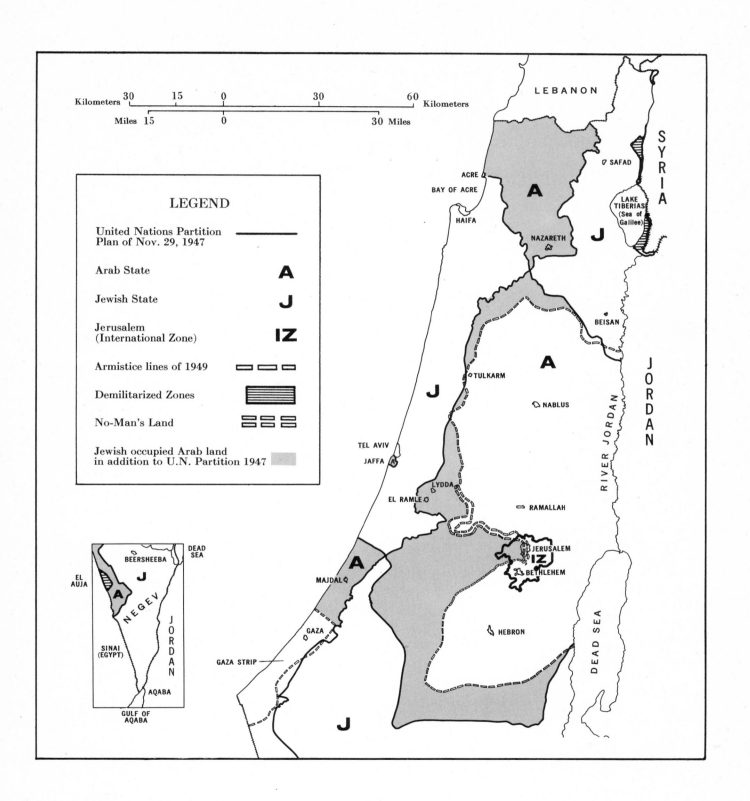

LEGEND

United Nations Partition
Plan of Nov. 29, 1947

Arab State **A**

Jewish State **J**

Jerusalem
(International Zone) **IZ**

Armistice lines of 1949

Demilitarized Zones

No-Man's Land

Jewish occupied Arab land
in addition to U.N. Partition 1947

They are human too . . .

They are human too . . . / PHOTOGRAPHIC DATA

PAGE 9. GAZA
Hasselblad 1000F with Tessar 80 m/m. 1/100 at 5.6 on Ilford HP 3 rated ASA 800 and developed in Microphen.

15. SAMIEHA
Hasselblad 100F with Ektar 135 m/m. 1/25 at 4 on Kodak Plus X rated ASA 400, developed in Microphen.

17. SAMIEHA
Leica M3 with 50 m/m Summarit. 1/100 at 2.8. Ilford HP 3 rated ASA 1000 and developed in Microphen.

19. SAMIEHA
Hasselblad with 80 m/m Tessar, 1/50 at 8 on Ilford HP 3 rated ASA 800 and developed in Microphen.

21. AMENT B'ALLAH
Hasselblad with 80 m/m Ektar, 1/250 at 5.6 with yellow Wratten filter on Ilford HP 3, rated ASA 1000, developed in Microphen.

26. RASH LITTLE BOYS . . .
Hasselblad, 80 m/m Ektar, 1/100 at 16 with orange Wratten filter. Kodak Plus X rated ASA 400. Developed in Microphen.

29. CHILDREN
Hasselblad with 80 m/m Ektar, 1/100 at 5.6. Kodak Plus X rated ASA 400 and developed in Microphen.

30-31. WOMEN
Bedouin girl; Hasselblad with Tessar 80 m/m 1/100 at 11, Plus X rated ASA 400, developed in Microphen.
Smiling girl with shawl; top, Hasselblad with 80 m/m Tessar, 1/100 at 16 on Kodak Plus X rated ASA 400, developed in Microphen. Women with half-covered face; middle, Hasselblad with Ektar 80 m/m, 1/250 at 16 on Plus X rated ASA 400, developed in Microphen. Embroidering girl; bottom, Hasselblad with 135 m/m Ektar, 1/100 at 11 on Plus X and developed in Microphen.

32. IN A CAFE
Leica M3 with Summarex 85 m/m. Ilford HPS 1/25 at 1.5. ASA rating 2600, developed in diluted Promicrol.

33. ALONG THE TRACKS
Hasselblad with Ektar 80 m/m. 1/250 at 8 with orange filter. Ilford HP 3 rated at ASA 1200 and developed in Promicrol.

34. MY FUTURE?
Hasselblad with Ektar 135 m/m. 1/100 at 11, yellow Wratten filter. Kodak Plus X, rated ASA 400 and developed in Microphen.

35. . . . AND MINE?
Hasselblad, Ektar 135 m/m. 1/100 at 16 on Kodak Plus X, rated ASA 400. Developed in Microphen.

36. A GAME
Hasselblad with Ektar 80 m/m. 1/250 at 8 on Ilford HP 3, rated ASA 1000 and developed in Promicrol.

37. KHAN YUNIS CAMP
Hasselblad, Tessar 80 m/m. 1/250 at 22 on Kodak Plus X, rated ASA 400 and developed in Microphen.

38. MET ON THE TRAIN EL ARISH—GAZA
1/500 at 16 on Ilford HP 3, rated ASA 1200. Developed in Promicrol. Hasselblad with Tessar 80 m/m.

39. THROUGH GAZA-STRIP
Hasselblad with Tessar 80 m/m. 1/250 at 22 and orange Wratten filter. Ilford HP 3 rated ASA 1200. Developed in Promicrol.

40-41. FAITH
Hasselblad, Tessar 80 m/m. 1/100 at 16 with yellow Wratten filter. Kodak Plus X, rated at 400 ASA. Developed in Microphen.

43. EFFORT TO SMILE
Hasselblad with Sonnar 250 m/m.-4. 1/100 at 11 and light yellow filter. Ilford HP 3 rated 1200 ASA, developed in Promicrol.

44. OLD PALESTINE ARAB REFUGEE WOMAN
Hasselblad with Ektar 80 m/m., 1/100 at 11 on Kodak Plus X rated ASA 400. Yellow Wratten filter. Developed in Microphen.

45. OLD PALESTINE ARAB REFUGEE
Hasselblad with Ektar 80 m/m., 1/100 at 16 on Ilford FP 3 rated ASA 600. Developed in diluted Promicrol.

46. PALESTINE ARAB REFUGEE FAMILY, 1
Leica M3 with Summarit 50 m/m. Plus X rated 400 ASA. 1/250 at 11. Yellow filter. Developed in diluted Promicrol.

47. SALAAM ALEIKUM . . .
Hasselblad with Ektar 80 m/m. 1/100 at 5.6 on Kodak Plus X rated ASA 400. Developed in Microphen.

48. MARKET IN KHAN YUNIS CAMP
Hasselblad with Tessar 80 m/m. 1/150 at 22 on Kodak Plus X rated ASA 400. Yellow filter. Developed in Microphen.

49. WHO CAN AFFORD TO BUY?
Leica M3 with Summarit 50 m/m. 1/250 at 5.6 on Kodak Plus X, developed in Microphen. ASA rating 400.

50. MUSTAFA, MOHAMMED AND MYSELF
Hasselblad with Ektar 80 m/m. 1/100 at 22, light yellow Wratten filter. Ilford HP 3 rated at ASA 1200 and developed in Promicrol.

51. WATERMELONS FOR EXPORT
Hasselblad with Tessar 80 m/m. 1/250 at 22 on Ilford HP 3 rated at 1200 ASA. Developed in Promicrol.

52. WAITING . . .
Hasselblad with Ektar 135 m/m. Kodak Plus X rated at ASA 400, 1/50 at 5.6. Developed in Microphen.

52. ARAB WOMAN WITH JARS
Leica M3 with Summarex 85 m/m. 1/250 at 16 on Kodak Plus X, rated ASA 400 and developed in Microphen.

53. THEY PUT TO SEA
Leica M3, Elmar 50 m/m-Kodak Plus X, rated 400 ASA, 1/250 at 11 with light yellow filter. Developed in Microphen.

54. OFF THE BEACH
Hasselblad, Tessar 80 m/m., Kodak Plus X rated 400 ASA. 1/250 at 16, developed in Microphen.

55. BAREFOOT ON SHELLS
Hasselblad with Tessar 80 m/m., 1/100 at 16 on Kodak Plus X with light yellow filter. Rating ASA 400, developed in Microphen.

55. THE SUDANESE CAMEL CORPS
Hasselblad with Ektar 80 m/m., 1/250 at 16 on Ilford HP 3 rated at ASA 1200 and developed in Promicrol.

56-57. PALESTINE ARAB REFUGEE FAMILY, 2
Hasselblad, Tessar 80 m/m., 1/250 at 5.6 on Kodak Plus X rated ASA 400 and developed in Microphen.

58. RETURN FROM NIGHT'S FISHING
Before sunrise, handheld Hasselblad with Ektar 80 m/m., 1/5 second at 2.8. Kodak Plus X rated at ASA 400. Developed in Microphen.

PAGE 59. **LOADING ORANGES FOR EXPORT**
Hasselblad with Ektar 80 m/m., 1/250 at 8 with Kodak Plus X rated 400 ASA. Light yellow filter and developed in Microphen.

61. **BLIND WOMAN AND GRANDDAUGHTER**
Hasselblad with Tessar 80 m/m., 1/250 at 16 on Ilford HP 3 rated 1200 ASA and developed in Microphen.

62. **BEDOUIN GIRL OUTSIDE A BAKERY**
Hasselblad with Tessar 80 m/m., 1/100 at 11 on Kodak Plus X rated 400 ASA and developed in Microphen.

63. **HAPPY GIRL INSIDE A BAKERY**
Leica M3 with Summarit 50 m/m., 1/10 at 1.5 on Kodak Tri-X, rated ASA 2800 and pushed in diluted Promicrol.

64. **THE DAY'S SALES REPORT**
Hasselblad with Ektar 80 m/m., 1/100 at 22 on Ilford HP 3 rated 1200 ASA. Yellow filter. Developed in Promicrol.

65. **A NEWSPAPER BOY AT THE STATION**
Hasselblad with Tessar 80 m/m., 1/100 at 11 on Kodak Plus X rated 400 ASA. Developed in Kodak D23 diluted.

67. **GIRL WITH BASKET**
Hasselblad with Ektar 80 m/m., 1/250 at 8 on Kodak Plus X rated 400 ASA, developed in diluted Promicrol.

68. **WOMAN THRESHING**
Hasselblad with Tessar 80 m/m., 1/100 at 16 on Kodak Plus X rated 400 ASA and developed in Microphen. Yellow filter.

68. **ARAB PLOWING**
Hasselblad with 250 m/m. Sonnar, light red filter, Ilford HP 3 rated 1200 ASA and developed in diluted Promicrol. 1/25 at 8.

69. **WOMAN ON DONKEY**
Hasselblad with Tessar 80 m/m., 1/250 at 8 with yellow Wratten filter on Kodak Plus X rated at ASA 400. Developed in Microphen.

69. **YOU A STRANGER?**
Hasselblad with Ektar 80 m/m., 1/250 at 5.6 on Ilford FP 3 with yellow Wratten filter. ASA rating 600. Developed in Promicrol.

70. **SHY SCHOOL GIRL**
Available light in the classroom. Hasselblad with Ektar 80 m/m., 1/50 at 2.8 on Ilford HP 3 rated ASA 1800, pushed in diluted Promicrol for 22 minutes at 68 F.

71. **SAME LITTLE SCHOOL GIRL**
Available light in the classroom. Hasselblad with Ektar 80 m/m., 1/50 at 2.8 on Ilford HP 3 rated ASA 1800 and pushed in diluted Promicrol.

72-73 **JUSTICE—JUSTICE!**
Hasselblad with Ektar 80 m/m., 1/100 at 5.6 with Kodak Plus X. Rating 400 ASA and developed in Microphen.

75. **NEW METHOD IN ENGLISH . . .**
Hasselblad with Ektar 135 m/m., 1/50 at 11 on Ilford HP 3 rated at 1200 ASA. Developed in Promicrol.

76. **WOMAN SPINNING**
Leica M3 with Summarit 50 m/m., 1/25 at 4 on Kodak Plus X rated at ASA 400. Developed in Microphen.

76-77. **MAN SPINNING, 1**
Leica M3 with Summarit 50 m/m., 1/5 at 8 on Kodak Plus X, rated at ASA 400. Developed in Microphen.

77. **MAN SPINNING, 2**
Leica M3 with Summarit 50 m/m., 1/5 at 11 on Plus X, ASA 400, developed in Microphen.

78. **SUFFERING**
Hasselblad with Ektar 80 m/m., 1/100 at 11 on Kodak Plus X rated ASA 400 and developed in Microphen.

79. **A SMOKE**
Hasselblad with Ektar 80 m/m., on lens special electronic ringflash mounted. 1/25 at 22 on Kodak Plus X developed in DK 20.

81. **FRIENDS**
Hasselblad with Ektar 80 m/m., on lens special electronic ringflash mounted. 1/25 at 16, developed in Microphen.

82. **EDITOR AND PUBLISHER OF GAZA NEWSPAPER**
Leica M3 with Summarit 50 m/m., 1/25 at 8 on Ilford HP 3 rated at 1600 ASA Developed in diluted Promicrol.

83. **TEACHERS—PALESTINE ARAB REFUGEES TOO**
Hasselblad with Tessar 80 m/m., 1/150 at 8 on Ilford HP 3 rated ASA 1000. Developed in Promicrol.

84-85. **REFLECTED IN MY EYES . . .**
Hasselblad with Ektar 80 m/m., 1/250 at 5.6 on Kodak Plus X, rated at ASA 400 and developed in diluted Promicrol.

86. **REFUGEE—RAILROAD— WORKMAN**
Hasselblad with Tessar 80 m/m., 1/25 at 2.8 on Ilford HPS, rated ASA 1800 and pushed in diluted Promicrol.

86. **BETWEEN EL ARISH AND GAZA**
Leica M3 with 50 m/m Elmar, 1/250 at 16 on Kodak Plus X, rated ASA 400. Developed in Microphen.

87. **ON THE TRAIN—A FRIENDLY SMILE . . .**
Leica M3 with Summarit 50 m/m., 1/250 at 2 on Kodak Plus X rated 400 ASA. Developed in Microphen.

88-89. **SHEPHERDS WITH SHEEP AND GOATS**
Leica M3 with Summarit 50 m/m., 1/100 at 8 on Ilford HPS rated at 1600 ASA and pushed in Promicrol.

91. **THE TRAIN IN GAZA— SYMBOLIC**
Hasselblad with Tessar 80 m/m., 1/100 at 16 on Ilford HP 3 rated ASA 1200 and developed in Promicrol.

Smoke and dirt in foreground for the life and misery of the Palestine Arab refugees; stopped train for impossibility of moving over to homeland, occupied, Palestine; sunlight in background for their homes on the other side of the demarcation line.

PAGE 93. EIGHT YEARS OLD
Hasselblad with Ektar 80 m/m., 1/50 at 5.6 on Kodak Plus X, rated ASA 400. Developed in diluted Promicrol.

94. LIFE IN MISERY
Hasselblad with 135 m/m. Ektar, 1/100 at 8 on Kodak Plus X rated 400 ASA. Developed in Microphen.

95. CLOSE TO NO-MAN'S LAND WHERE THE TRACKS END
Leica M3 with 50 m/m. Summarit. 1/5 at 4 on Ilford HP 3 rated at 1200 ASA. Developed in Promicrol.

96. FROM WHERE?—NAZARETH
Hasselblad with Tessar 80 m/m., Electronic ringflash mounted on the lens. 1/25 at 22, developed in diluted Promicrol.

97. HIS DAUGHTER
Hasselblad with Tessar 80 m/m. Electronic ringflash w. max. output 480 joules, min. output 90 joules. Mounted on lens. 1/25 at 16, developed in diluted Promicrol.

98-99. PALESTINE ARAB REFUGEES IN GAZA BEACH CAMP
Hasselblad with Ektar 80 m/m., 1/100 at 16 on Kodak Plus X, rated 400 ASA and developed in Microphen.

100. ARAB WOMAN OUTSIDE HER CAMP MUD HUT
Hasselblad with Ektar 80 m/m., 1/100 at 16 on Kodak Plus X rated ASA 400. Developed in Microphen.

101. IN THE MUD HUT—ENTRANCE
Hasselblad with Tessar 80 m/m., 1/100 at 22 on Ilford HP 3, rated ASA 1000. Developed in Microphen.

102. TWO WOMEN WITH JARS
Hasselblad with 250 m/m Sonnar, light red filter, 1/100 at 8 on Ilford HP 3 rated at ASA 1000. Developed in diluted Promicrol.

103. WOMAN WITH JAR
Hasselblad with Ektar 80 m/m. 1/250 at 11 on Kodak Plus X rated at ASA 400 and developed in Microphen.

104-105. WOMAN WITH JAR—SILHOUETTE
Leica M3 with Summarit 50 m/m. 1/500 at 11 on Ilford HP 3 rated ASA 1200 and developed in diluted Promicrol. Picture is one third of negative.

107. 1500 CALORIES A DAY . . .
Hasselblad with Ektar 80 m/m., 1/250 at 5.6 on Kodak Plus X rated at ASA 400 and developed in Microphen.

108. BOY WITH BASKET
Hasselblad with Tessar 80 m/m., 1/100 at 8 on Kodak Plus X rated 400 ASA. Developed in diluted Microphen.

109. A NEW DRESS
Hasselblad, 135 m/m Ektar, 1/100 at 11 on HP 3 rated at 1200 ASA and developed in diluted Promicrol.

110. WOMAN WITH COVERED FACE
Hasselblad with Ektar 135 m/m., 1/100 at 16 on Kodak Plus X and developed in Microphen. Film rating ASA 400.

111. GIRL CARRYING FOOD FOR HER CHICKEN
Hasselblad with Tessar 80 m/m., 1/250 at 5.6 on Kodak Plus X. Film rated at ASA 400 and developed in Microphen.

113. OLD MAN WITH STICK
Hasselblad with Ektar 80 m/m., 1/100 at 11 on Ilford HP 3 rated at ASA 1000. Developed in diluted Promicrol.

114-115. SMILING BOY
Leica M3 with Summarit 50 m/m., 1/100 at 4 on Ilford HP 3, rated ASA 1000 and developed in diluted Promicrol.

116. A SILENT FACE
Hasselblad with Ektar 80 m/m, 1/100 at 16 on Ilford HP 3 rated 1200 ASA and developed in diluted Promicrol.

118. THE BLIND BEGGAR
Hasselblad, Tessar 80 m/m., 1/100 at 11 on Kodak Plus X, rated 400 ASA. Developed in Microphen.

119. THE BLIND BEGGAR
Leica M3 with Elmar 50 m/m., 1/50 at 8 on Kodak Plus X developed in Microphen. Film rating ASA 400.

120-121. 12 YEARS OLD—PROUD AND STRANGE
Hasselblad, Tessar 80 m/m., 1/25 at 4. Early morning, before sunrise. Kodak Plus X rated at ASA 400 and developed in Microphen.

122. GIRL ON THE BEACH
Hasselblad, Ektar 80 m/m., 1/100 at 22 on Ilford HP 3 with yellow Wratten filter. Film rating ASA 1000. Developed in diluted Promicrol.

122-123. FISHES IN NET
Hasselblad, Ektar 80 m/m., 1/100 at 16 with orange Wratten filter. Film rating ASA 1000, developed in Microphen.

124-125. BOY AT THE BEACH
Hasselblad, Tessar 80 m/m., 1/25 at 5.6. One hour before sunrise. Kodak Plus X rated 400 ASA and developed in Microphen.

126. Same as page 122-123.
127. BOY WITH NET
Hasselblad, Ektar 80 m/m, 1/100 at 16 with orange Wratten filter. HP 3 rated ASA 1000 and developed in diluted Promicrol.

128-129. WAITING FOR FOOD RATIONS
Leica M3, Summarit 50 m/m., 1/100 at 5.6 on Kodak Plus X rated ASA 400 and developed in Microphen.

130-131. IN AN UNRWA FEEDING CENTER
Leica M3 with Summarit 50 m/m., 1/25 at 4. Ilford HP 3 rated 1000 ASA and developed in diluted Promicrol.

132-133. WHAT ABOUT HIS FUTURE?
Leica M3, 50 m/m. Summarit, 1/10 at 1.5 on Kodak Plus X rated ASA 400. Developed in Microphen.

134. RESIGNATION
Hasselblad, 135 m/m Ektar, 1/100 at 5.6 on Kodak Plus X rated at ASA 400. Developed in D 23.

135. GIRL IN SCHOOL
Hasselblad with Ektar 80 m/m., Ilford HP 3 rated ASA 1200 1/100 at 2,8 and developed in diluted Promicrol.

135. BOY IN SCHOOL
Hasselblad, Tessar 80 m/m., 1/10 at 2.8—handheld camera. Ilford HP 3, rated ASA 1000 and developed in diluted Promicrol.

136-137. PALESTINE ARAB REFUGEE FAMILY, 3
Hasselblad, Tessar 80 m/m., 1/250 at 11—from the train. Kodak Plus X rated 400 ASA and developed in Microphen.

138. MOTHER AND CHILD—BEDOUINS
Hasselblad, Ektar 80 m/m., 1/100 at 16 on Kodak Plus X, developed in Promicrol.

139. MOTHER AND CHILD— BEDOUINS

Hasselblad, Ektar 80 m/m., special electronic ring flash mounted on the lens. 1/25 at 11 on Kodak Plus X, developed in Promicrol.

141. THE CUTE LITTLE GIRL

Hasselblad, Ektar 135 m/m., 1/50 at 8 on Kodak Plus X rated ASA 400 and developed in Microphen.

142-143. ANOTHER SCHOOL BOY

Hasselblad, Tessar 80 m/m., 1/10 at 4, handheld camera. Kodak Plus X 400 ASA, developed in Microphen.

144. ANOTHER SCHOOL GIRL

Hasselblad, Tessar 80 m/m., 1/25 at 2.8—handheld camera. Ilford HP 3 rated ASA 1000 and developed in diluted Promicrol.

146-147. HARD LABOR—PAID 8 CENTS A DAY . . .

Hasselblad, Ektar 80 m/m., 1/250 at 8 on Kodak Plus X rated ASA 400 and developed in Microphen. Yellow filter.

149. BORN TO BE A PALESTINE REFUGEE

Leica M3, Summarit 50 m/m., 1/50 at 1.5 on HP 3 rated ASA 1200. Developed in diluted Promicrol.

150-151. SYMBOLIC

Leaves for their farms in occupied Palestine—sunlighted area for Palestine—shadowed area for their present area—refugee's shadow falling into occupied Palestine.

Shot from train with Hasselblad, Tessar 80 m/m at 1/250 at 16 with yellow Wratten filter on Ilford HP 3 rated ASA 1200. Developed in Promicrol.

152-153. ON THE MARKET IN GAZA CITY

Leica M3 with Summarit 50 m/m., 1/50 at 11 on Ilford FP 3 rated ASA 600 and developed in diluted Promicrol.

154-155. FARMER IN HIS HOMELAND, WAR VICTIM, NOW SHOEMAKER

Leica M3, Summarit 50 m/m., 1/100 at 11 on Kodak Plus X rated at ASA 400. Developed in Microphen.

156. NIHAD THE ARTIST— REFUGEE FROM JAFFA

Hasselblad, Ektar 80 m/m., 1/50 at 5.6 on Ilford FP 3, rated at ASA 600 and developed in diluted Promicrol.

157. HAVE YOUR PICTURE TAKEN!

Bottom left. Hasselblad, Tessar 80 m/m., 1/100 at 11 on Kodak Plus X rated 400 ASA and developed in D 23.

157. HRANT THE STUDIO PHOTOGRAPHER—REFUGEE FROM JAFFA

Top right. Hasselblad, Ektar 80 m/m. 1/25 at 2.8 on Ilford HP 3 rated ASA 1200 and developed in D 76.

158. ANOTHER OLD MAN . . .

Hasselblad, Ektar 80 m/m., 1/50 at 8 on Kodak Plus X rated ASA 400 and developed in Microphen. Light red filter.

159. BARBERS' SHOP IN KHAN YUNIS CAMP

Hasselblad with Tessar 80 m/m., 1/100 at 8 on Kodak Plus X, rating ASA 400 and developed in D 23.

161. EXPECTING THE BLACK ANGEL . . .

Hasselblad, Ektar 80 m/m., 1/25 at 4 on Ilford HP 3, rated ASA 1000 and developed in diluted Promicrol.

162-163. OLD MAN IN TB HOSPITAL WARD

Three pix. Leica M3 with Summarit 50 m/m., 1/100 at 2.8 on Kodak Tri X, film rating ASA 1600. Developed in diluted Promicrol.

164. TB IS BRED IN THE CAMPS . . .

Leica M3, Summarit 50 m/m., 1/25 at 2 on Tri-X, rating ASA 1600 and developed in diluted Promicrol.

165. I RETURNED 2 MONTHS LATER: SHE WAS DEAD—TB

Leica M3, Summarit 50 m/m., 1/25 at 2 on Tri-X rated 1600 ASA and developed in diluted Promicrol.

166-167. THE SCHOOL IN THE TB HOSPITAL

Leica M3, Elmar 50 m/m., 1/100 at 8 on Kodak Plus X rated at ASA 400. Developed in Microphen.

168-169. WAITING FOR THEIR TB ADDITIONAL FOOD RATION . . .

Leica M3, Summarit 50 m/m., 1/250 at

5.6. Tri-X rated 1600 ASA. Developed in diluted Promicrol.

170. IN A TB WARD

Leica M3, Summarit 50 m/m., 1/100 at 5.6 on Tri-X, rated 1600 ASA. Developed in diluted Promicrol.

171. ANOTHER OLD MAN IN A TB WARD

Hasselblad, Ektar 80 m/m., 1/25 at 2.8 on Ilford HP 3 rated 1000 ASA and developed in diluted Promicrol.

172. MORNING WASH IN CHILDREN'S TB WARD

Leica M3 with Summarit 50 m/m., 1/25 at 8 on Tri-X rated 1600 ASA and developed in diluted Promicrol.

173. NO HOPE—ONE AND A HALF LUNG CLOSED

Hasselblad with Ektar 80 m/m., 1/25 at 4 on Ilford HP 3 rated 1000 ASA. Developed in diluted Promicrol.

174-175. STILL HOPE?

Leica M3 with 50 m/m Summarit. 1/50 at 4 on Kodak Tri-X rated 1600 ASA and developed in diluted Promicrol.

177. WILL SHE STAY ALIVE?

Hasselblad with Ektar 80 m/m., 1/100 at 2.8 on Ilford HP 3, film rating ASA 1000 and developed in diluted Promicrol.

178. LIFE MIRRORED IN HIS EYES . . .

Hasselblad, Ektar 80 m/m, 1/50 at 4 on Ilford HP 3 rated 1000 ASA and developed in diluted Promicrol.

181. TB AND STARVATION . . . 18 MONTHS OLD

Hasselblad, Tessar 80 m/m., 1/25 at 4 on Kodak Plus X rated 400 ASA and developed in D 23.

182. HANDS . . .

Hasselblad, 250 m/m Sonnar with red filter. Picture is fraction of negative. 1/25 at 5.6 on Ilford HP 3 rated ASA 1600 and developed in D 76.

183. CRYING WIDOW

Hasselblad, 250 m/m Sonnar. Same negative as page 182.

184-185. REFUGEE WIDOW AT BEACH CEMETERY

Hasselblad with 250 m/m. Sonnar, red filter. Ilford HP 3 rated ASA 1600 and developed in D 76. Pix shot few minutes before dawn.